101 American Superstitions

Understanding Language and Culture Through Superstitions

Harry Collis

Illustrated by Joe Kohl

PASSPORT BOOKS

NTC/Contemporary Publishing Company

Editorial Director: Cindy Krejcsi
Executive Editor: Mary Jane Maples
Editors: Jim Harmon, Michael O'Neill
Design Manager: Ophelia M. Chambliss
Cover and Interior Design: Karen Christoffersen
Cover Illustration: Joe Kohl
Production Manager: Margo Goia

Acknowledgments
My deep appreciation goes to my editors, Jim Harmon, Michael O'Neill, and Barbara Moreland, for
their contributions and suggestions in the preparation of the manuscript of this work.

ISBN: 0-8442-5599-8

Contents

Foreword

Although superstitions have their origins in the beliefs and practices of the past, they continue to flourish even in the most technologically advanced societies. They are alive and well because individuals continue to believe that there is a power beyond themselves that can account for or influence the course of a situation over which they have little or no control.

In the past the fear of the unknown led to a strong belief in unseen spirits—most of whom were evil. To appease these evil powers, people invented all sorts of charms and spells as "antidotes" that could be depended on either to bring good luck or to ward off bad luck and, most importantly, dispel the fear of the unknown.

Although the beliefs and practices of superstitions are based on neither reason nor fact, superstitions steadfastly remain a part of the language and background of people of all nations since they are an outgrowth of things that are important in everyone's daily existence—food, work, money, interpersonal relations, and so on. For this reason, the superstitions contained in *101 American Superstitions* will spark lively student discussions on the similarities in, and variations on, the same themes in the culture or folklore of their native countries.

101 American Superstitions is designed to help students understand the culture and English of the United States by reading about common superstitions. The superstitions in this book are grouped into nine thematic sections in order to help students understand the contexts in which they arise. Accompanied by a humorous illustration, each superstition is followed by a short dialogue or narrative that contextualizes it and clarifies its meaning. In short, *101 American Superstitions* provides a fun way to enjoy English and learn it at the same time.

So if you believe that you should not step on a crack, walk under a ladder, or open an umbrella inside a house, you are in good company. Do you also knock on wood, throw salt over your left shoulder, say *gesundheit* when someone sneezes, or carry a rabbit's foot for good luck? Indeed, we might ask, "Is there actually some truth to superstitions?" If we consider them as a way to alleviate our fears or bolster our hopes in the face of adversity, the answer may be yes.

Come to think of it, washing the car *does* seem to bring on rain.

Section One
Body Language

1 If you sing before seven, you will cry before eleven

There's an old belief that the morning is too early to be happy. Happiness has to be earned each day—otherwise, you are sure to have bad luck.

A: (singing) Oh, what a beautiful morning!
B: Do you really want that new job?
A: Of course I do!
B: Then you'd better not act too happy, at least before noon.

2 Asking God's blessing for a sneezer

People once believed the soul could escape from the body when a person sneezed. To stop this from happening, people ask God to bless—and so to protect—the person who sneezes.

A: Ah chu! (loud sneeze)
B: God bless you!
A: Thanks. I sure could use His blessing. I feel a cold coming on.

3 Stopping hiccups

It was once believed that a person with hiccups was possessed by the devil. Many remedies are supposed to stop hiccups, such as scaring the person or having the person hold her nose while drinking water.

Sally couldn't get her daughter to stop hiccuping. She tried to scare her by making a loud noise. When that didn't work she had her daughter take small drinks of water while holding her nose. At last, the hiccups stopped.

4 **Cover your mouth when you yawn**

An old superstition says that yawning is caused by the devil and that evil spirits enter the body when your mouth is open wide. Covering your mouth stops them. Now, it is simply considered rude not to cover your mouth when you yawn. It is also believed that watching someone else yawn will cause you to yawn too.

A: Oh, I just can't stop yawning.
B: At least you could cover your mouth!
A: Sorry. I didn't mean to be so rude, but I've been studying since early this morning.
B: I know, but yawning is catching. If you don't stop, I'll soon start.

5 An itchy nose predicts a quarrel

There are many superstitions about itching. For example, an itchy nose means you're going to have a quarrel with someone.

A: I'll see you later.

B: Where are you going? You just got here.

A: Yeah, and in the five minutes I've been here you've scratched your nose a dozen times. I'm in no mood for a quarrel.

6 Spitting on your hands for strength

Seeing animals licking their wounds caused people to believe that saliva had some magical healing power. Even today the first thing someone does when they hurt their finger is put it in their mouth. Nowadays, when we spit on our hands, we are asking for added strength.

A: Boy, you must be quite strong to handle chopping up all that wood.
B: Actually, spitting on my hands gives me the strength to do the job.
A: That's some pile you've got there. Let's hope your saliva lasts long enough to chop it all up.

7 Getting rid of a cough

People have tried many strange remedies to get rid of a cough. One cure is to take a hair from the coughing person's head, put it between two slices of buttered bread, feed it to a dog, and say, "Eat well you hound. May you be sick and I be sound."

A: You've been coughing all night. Have you taken any medicine?
B: Yes, I've tried all kinds of medicines. Nothing worked.
A: I know what to do. I'll find a dog. You get some bread and butter.
B: You and your ridiculous cures! Frankly, I'd prefer something hot to drink.

8 Curing cramps

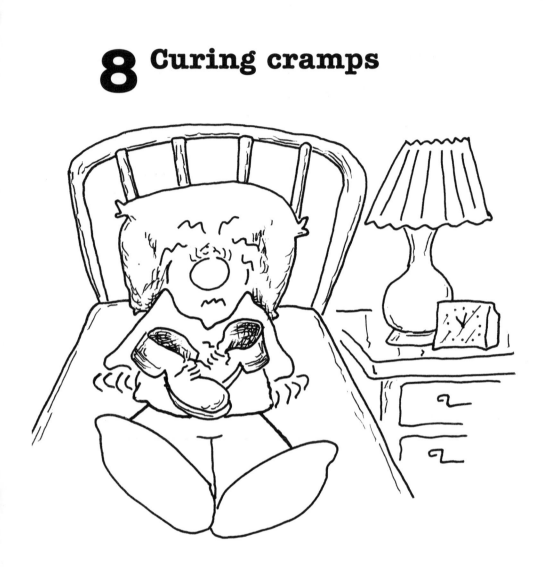

Superstition says that one way to stop the pain of a cramp is by carrying certain animal bones on your body. Another cure is to lay your shoes on your stomach, across the cramp.

Little Johnny had stomach cramps after eating too many cookies and sweets at the party. When medicine didn't work, Johnny's mother tried an old cure her grandmother had used. When his father came home, Johnny was asleep—with his shoes on his stomach!

9 Cross your fingers to make a wish come true

It is said that bad luck is trapped at the point where the two fingers meet. So when we cross our fingers, we stop the bad luck from escaping and allow our wishes to come true.

A: Congratulations! I heard that you got that job in the department store.
B: Not yet, but I hope to hear soon.
A: Well, I'll keep my fingers crossed for you.
B: Thanks. I need all the good luck I can get.

10 Whistling brings misfortune

People used to think that whistling was the noise made by evil spirits and that it invited misfortune. Whistling was considered very unlucky in a closed place such as a house or a ship. It was considered especially unlucky, for example, to whistle in a theater dressing room.

A: Mary, stop your whistling right now!

B: But Mom, I'm just whistling while we clean. I'm happy and excited about the party.

A: But it's bad luck to whistle in the house. Do you want to ruin your father's birthday?

B: OK, I'll stop. I don't want anything to go wrong at the party.

11 Pulling out a gray hair will cause more to grow

People have always thought that hair had magical powers, and there are many superstitions about human hair. One belief is that pulling out a single gray or white hair will cause ten more to grow in its place.

John got angry every time he looked in the mirror and saw a new gray hair. But he was afraid to pull out even one because he believed that if he did, he would grow even more gray.

12 Fingernail clippings must not be left for others to find

An old American belief says that fingernails can by used to cast spells on their owner. The clippings must never be left around for the evil spirits to find. To be safe they should be burned or buried.

A: I can't believe all the things that have gone wrong since I broke up with my girlfriend. I lost my car keys, my TV was stolen, and I have a terrible cold.

B: Maybe she put a spell on you to get even.

A: How could she do that?

B: Well, you know how she hated to find your fingernail clippings on the floor. Maybe she used them to call out the evil spirits.

13 The evil eye

There is an ancient belief that some people have the power to harm another's health or happiness simply by looking at them. To protect yourself from being noticed by the evil eye, you must not openly praise yourself or call attention to any good fortune.

A: Hey, I got 100 on my test! That's the highest score in the whole school. Now I get to go to the next competition, and my teacher says I have a good chance to win.

B: Not so loud, or you'll end up losing if the evil eye notices your good fortune.

Section Two
Love and Marriage

14 Carrying the bride across the threshold

The custom of the groom carrying his bride over the threshold is believed to bring the couple good fortune. One superstition says that evil spirits trying to spoil the newlyweds' happiness might cause the bride to fall as she enters her new home, so the groom should carry her to keep her from falling.

A couple had just come back from their honeymoon, and the husband was eager to surprise his bride with the new stereo equipment that he had purchased for their apartment. So he picked her up and told her to close her eyes as he carried her across the threshold. He hoped she would be pleased when she saw the compact discs of her favorite music as well.

15 Something old, something new, something borrowed, something blue

When getting married, brides traditionally wear or carry something old, something new, something borrowed, and something blue. "Something old" can be anything that has brought good luck to its owner in the past. "Something new" is a symbol of hope for the future. "Something borrowed" adds the good luck of the giver to the bride. And blue, considered a lucky color, is a traditional protection for all women.

A: Anna, the ceremony is about to begin. Are you ready?

B: Yes. I'm wearing my grandmother's necklace (old) and my beautiful wedding gown (new). Dad's lucky penny (borrowed) is tied into my bouquet with a blue ribbon (blue). Everything is perfect.

16 Cutting the wedding cake

The wedding cake has always stood for good fortune and fertility. The bride, with the help of her groom, must cut the first piece as a sign that they will share all possessions in the future.

A: That wedding cake looks delicious, and I'm hungry. Let's go get some.

B: Don't you go near that cake! You know we must wait for the bride and groom to cut the first piece for themselves. It's tradition.

17 Choosing the wedding date

The Romans believed that Juno, their goddess of women, blessed marriages that took place in her month. So June is considered the perfect month for marriage.

A: Lisa, have you decided on a date for your wedding?
B: We're not sure yet, but sometime in the summer. I've always dreamed of a June wedding. They seem so perfect.
A: Yes. My parents were married in June, and they've been together for 35 years.

18 The groom must not see the bride before the wedding

Among the many superstitions concerning the wedding ceremony is the custom that the groom must not see his bride before the wedding ceremony. To do so would be a sign of submission to her family.

A: Hey, Phil. I saw Marilyn as she was entering the church. She looks beautiful.

B: I'm sure she is. Her sisters wouldn't let me anywhere near her today.

A: Well, you don't want to spoil anything. And you don't have to wait much longer. The music has just started.

19 Throwing the bridal bouquet

The bridal bouquet has traditionally been a symbol of
fertility. Throwing the bouquet is a modern addition to
the wedding ceremony that says the woman who catches
it will be the next one to marry.

A: Now Jessica is the only one of our school friends who isn't married.
B: Yes, but I heard she and Tom are talking about marriage.
A: That's great. If she catches the bride's bouquet, we'll know for
sure there's another wedding ahead.

20 Wearing a veil

The wedding veil is a reminder of the bridal canopy that was built to keep the evil eye from the wedding celebration. Raising the veil is a symbol of the daughter's freedom from her parents' control.

The bride looked so small and young with the lace veil covering her face. But when the groom lifted it to kiss his bride, we saw a woman ready to build a new life with her husband.

21 Wearing a wedding ring

In earlier times a wife was considered a possession, and the wedding ring was a sign that she had been purchased by the groom. The giving of the ring sealed the agreement.

A: Have you picked out your wedding ring yet?
B: We've decided on mine, but we haven't found the right one for Bill.
A: I thought only the woman wore a ring.
B: What an old-fashioned idea! Bill isn't buying me. Rings mean that we give ourselves to each other.

22 Throwing rice

Throwing rice at newlyweds was traditionally a way to wish them many children. In places where rice was the basic food, couples needed many children to grow and harvest it. Nowadays, throwing rice at the bride and groom is a way to wish them a happy marriage.

When Stephanie and Paul left the church, their guests followed them out and began throwing rice. Stephanie knew that the guests were simply wishing them a happy marriage, but her mother hoped the wishes also meant many grandchildren.

23 The honeymoon is over

The word **honeymoon** comes from the custom that
newlyweds were to drink mead and honey for the first
thirty days after their marriage as the moon went
through all of its phases. After those thirty days the
couple's love was believed to wane, like the moon.

A: Hello, John. Nice to have you back at the office. How was the
   honeymoon?
B: Wonderful. And Sara and I had a really relaxing time on the
   beach. But now we have to get back to work and responsibilities.
A: Yes, I guess the honeymoon is over.
B: Well, not completely!

24 Protectors of the wedding couple

The bridesmaids and ushers once dressed like the bride and groom to trick evil spirits so that they would not know who was getting married. Later, the job of the ushers was to stand watch during the honeymoon. Nowadays, bridesmaids and ushers are simply friends who help the bride and groom during the wedding celebration.

A: Virginia, have you picked out your bridesmaids yet?
B: Yes, I have. I've asked five of my best friends, and Bill is asking five cousins to be ushers.
A: Wow! That's a large wedding party.
B: Maybe, but for such a special day we want all the help we can get.

25 Orange blossoms for eternal love

Orange blossoms are often found in the bridal bouquet. The orange blossom tree represents eternal love and so is a perfect symbol for a wedding.

A: Silvia, have you chosen the flowers for your bridal bouquet?
B: Not completely, but I know I want to use orange blossoms. They are so beautiful and smell so wonderful.
A: For sure. And they always make me think of lovers.

26 Wearing a white wedding gown

As far back as the Greeks, the white gown was a symbol of joy. Now a white wedding dress is more a symbol of purity than of joy.

Now that Marie was getting married, she did not need to go searching for the perfect gown. She decided to wear the same white gown her mother had worn as a young bride.

27 The wedding kiss

The wedding kiss is the sign of the holy pledge between the bride and groom. According to tradition, it is lucky for the bride to cry at this point in the ceremony. If she does not, there will be tears throughout the marriage.

A: What a wonderful wedding!
B: They look so happy. Did you notice that when they faced the guests after their kiss, both the bride and groom had tears in their eyes and big smiles on their faces?
A: Yes, their marriage is off to a good start.

28 Tying old shoes to the newlyweds' car

This custom began in a time when the father of the bride gave her old shoes to the groom as a symbol that he was now responsible for her care.

A: What a racket the couple's car made when they drove away!

B: It's no wonder with all those tin cans tied to the rear fender. But what were those old shoes doing there?

A: Maybe someone thought they'd come in handy if the car ran out of gas.

Section Three
Food for Thought

29 Eat apples for good health

Apples have long been connected to superstitions about health, love, and death. Nowadays, a common belief is that the apple will bring good health to the person who eats it. A well-known American saying is "An apple a day keeps the doctor away."

A: Mom, these apples are really good! This is the second one I've had today.

B: I'm glad you like them. It's better to spend money on healthy food than on a visit to the doctor.

30 Saying "bread and butter" to avoid separation

Superstition has it this way: Bread that has been buttered can never be unbuttered. So when two people walking together are parted by something, they say "bread and butter" to be sure nothing separates their friendship.

Pam and Jill were walking home from school together, just as they did every day. As they came to the mailbox on the corner, Pam moved to the left and Jill to the right. Both girls laughed and said, "Bread and butter."

31 Never leave an eggshell unbroken

According to an old superstition, once an egg is eaten, it is important to break up the shell completely. If you don't, a witch may use the empty shell as a boat, set sail in it, and destroy ships at sea.

A: Dad, why do you break up the shells after you cook your eggs?
B: My father was a sailor. My mother always broke egg shells completely and said doing that helped protect him when he was at sea. He always came home safely, so I'm still wishing sailors good luck.

32 Do not return an empty food container

If one is given a gift of food, the container it came in must not be returned empty. To return it empty would bring hunger to the house of the giver or the receiver.

A: Tommy, will you take this plate of cookies to Jim's house for me?

B: Why are you sending cookies to them?

A: Jim's mother sent that plate filled with candy to my birthday party. I can't send it back empty.

33 Do not throw away unwanted bread

Since bread is a basic food of most people, superstition says that it is wrong to throw away unwanted bread. Those who do will go hungry.

A: Beth, you can't throw that bread in the trash.
B: Why not? It's too stale to eat.
A: OK, but don't throw it away. Let's put it outside for the birds.

34 Taking the last piece of food

There is a superstition that warns us never to take the last piece of food on a plate. To do so means that we won't marry, or if we are married, we may soon find ourselves unmarried again.

The family laughed at young Michael because he ate so much. They said he would still be unmarried at 40 because at dinner he always took the last piece of meat and drank the last glass of milk.

35 Cure all ills with garlic

People have long believed in the healing powers of garlic. It was often hung in a home to help a sick person get well. It was also worn around a healthy person's neck to protect against illness.

A: What is that terrible smell?
B: It's me. My mother put this garlic around my neck.
A: Why would she do that?
B: She says I've been sick so much lately that she'll try anything to keep me healthy.

36 Spilt milk

Superstition says that spilling milk will bring seven days of bad luck because spirits will come to any house where they can find milk on the floor.

A: I knew this week would be terrible. My dog ran away, my bike broke, and my girlfriend dumped me.

B: Sure, you've had some bad luck, but how could you know these things would happen?

A: Because on Monday morning I spilled a big glass of milk on the kitchen floor. Boy, I'll sure be glad when this week is over.

37 Throwing salt over the left shoulder

Because humans and animals need salt for life, spilling salt was considered a serious misfortune and a sign that evil spirits were trying to take away the household's salt. To avoid them, you should throw a pinch of salt over your left shoulder because that is the side where the spirits live.

A: Mario, you've spilled salt all over the table. Now you're throwing it over your shoulder and onto the floor. Why are you making such a mess?

B: Spilling the salt on the table was an accident. Grandma says if I throw some over my shoulder I won't have any more accidents, and I'll always have salt for my food.

38 Eat fish for brain food and good fortune

It is commonly believed that eating fish is good for the brain. For good luck, fish should be eaten from head to tail.

A: Let's have lunch before our test. We need to eat lots of fish.

B: I'm hungry, too, but I don't like fish.

A: You better eat it anyway—from head to tail. I've heard this math test is really hard, and our brains need all the help they can get.

39 Pulling a wishbone

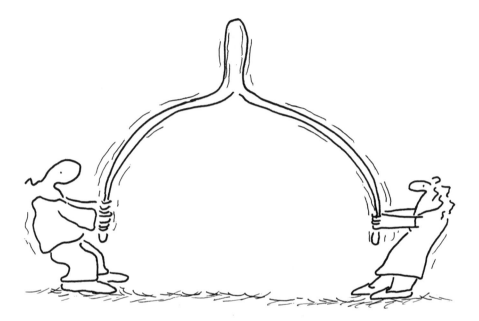

The forked bone that lies between the neck and breast of a bird is called the wishbone. When two people pull the bone until it breaks, the one holding the larger piece is given a wish. For the wish to come true, it must be kept secret.

A: Mom, Kevin isn't playing fair. He used two hands to pull on the wishbone.

B: But Sam is bigger than me. If I don't use two hands, he always wins. I want to wish for a puppy.

A: It won't matter. You told me your wish, so now it can't come true.

40 Using pepper to get rid of an unwanted guest

One tradition says that putting a little pepper under the chair of a guest will keep him from visiting too long.

A: How much longer is your brother going to stay? He's been here two weeks already.

B: I know. I'm ready for him to leave, too, but I don't want to be rude. When he sits down for dinner, I'll put some pepper under his chair. Maybe he'll take the hint.

41 Tea leaves tell the future

Many people claim that they can tell the future by reading the patterns tea leaves make when the empty cup has been turned upside down onto a saucer.

A: Have you heard the news? Larry is going to ask Anna to marry him.

B: That's great, but how do you know?

A: My grandmother read it in Anna's tea leaves.

Section Four
I've Got Your Number

42 Three on a match

There is a superstition that warns us never to light three cigarettes with one match. The belief comes from soldiers who knew that the light of the match could show the enemy where they were.

Charles and his friends were standing outside the store smoking cigarettes. George asked Charles for a light, but Charles refused. "I already lit cigarettes for John and me. I can't light a third with this match, and it's my last one."

43 All things come in threes

Because it represents the traditional family—mother, father, and child—three is thought to be lucky. Gifts, letters, and visitors come in threes. But it is said that bad events—like accidents and funerals—come in threes as well.

A: I'm so worried. I know I won't get that new job now.
B: What makes you think so?
A: Bad things always come in threes. My car broke down on Tuesday, and last night I lost my new necklace.
B: But yesterday you found five dollars, and you got an A on today's English test. Since good things also come in threes, tomorrow I'm sure you'll get that job.

44 Lucky three at the card table

To change their luck when they are losing, some card players get up from their chairs and spin them around three times before sitting down again. Others walk around the table three times before beginning to play.

A: Stop walking in circles, Bob. Sit down and let's play cards.

B: Just a minute; I need to go around one more time. Last week when we played, I lost the whole night. This week I'll do whatever it takes to win.

45 If you're born on the first day of the month

Many people believe that children born on the first day of the month will have good fortune throughout their lives. The number one is considered very lucky.

A: Goodness! What an active baby! He's so alert.
B: Thanks, Judith. Bill and I play a lot of games with him.
A: How old is he?
B: He'll be one on August 1st.
A: He sure is lucky! Born on the first of the month to parents who think he's the most important person in the world!

46 A two-dollar bill

In the United States the two-dollar bill is considered unlucky since it is a reminder of the two or **deuce** in a deck of playing cards; "deuce" is an old name for the devil. To change the bad luck, the corner of the bill should be torn off.

A: Paul, can you lend me some money?
B: All I have is this two-dollar bill. Do you want it?
A: Sure. I'll tear the corner to be safe. Then maybe I'll get lucky and my paycheck will come early.

47 Cats have nine lives

In ancient Egypt cats were believed to be like gods, and to kill a cat was a crime that could be punished by death. The modern belief that a cat has nine lives comes from this tradition.

A: I believe our cat must be the luckiest animal in the world.

B: What makes you think so?

A: She's been hit by a car three times now and has never been hurt seriously.

B: Then she's still got six accidents coming.

48 The seven-year itch

A common superstition says that the body and mind of every person changes every seven years. In American tradition this change is called the "seven-year itch."

Marilyn was unhappy with her job, her family, and her house. For seven years everything had been the same. Now she wanted something different. It was time to make changes in her everyday life. It was time to scratch that seven-year itch.

49 Thirteen at a table

Many traditions consider the number thirteen to be unlucky. One such superstition says that it is unlucky to be the thirteenth guest at a dinner table.

Jessica had invited sixteen people to her dinner party, but only thirteen were able to come. She was so afraid something would go wrong that at the last minute she invited her sister to be the fourteenth guest.

Section Five
Be Careful!

50 Stepping on a crack

An old saying goes, "Step on a crack; break your mother's back." A crack in the sidewalk represented the opening of a grave, and stepping on a crack meant inviting death to your family.

Six-year-old Mary walked slowly along the sidewalk, looking down at her feet.
"Hurry up, Mary," her father said. "What are you looking at?"
"I have to go slowly and watch for cracks. Sammy stepped on a crack, and now his mother's in the hospital. I don't want anything to happen to Mommy."

51 Walking under a ladder

A ladder leaning against a wall forms a triangle with the wall and the earth. According to traditional belief, the three sides of the triangle represent the family, so passing through the triangle destroys the wholeness of the family. This belief is the root of the superstition that walking under a ladder brings bad luck.

A: Stop! You're not going to walk under that ladder, are you?
B: Surely you don't believe that old superstition.
A: I do now. Last month I walked under a ladder, and two days later my sister took a new job and moved 300 miles away.

52 A black cat crossing your path

People used to believe witches could change themselves into cats. A black cat crossing your path is bad luck because it might really be a witch.

A: Pam, why are you crying?

B: I knew something terrible would happen when that black cat crossed in front of me on the way to school this morning. I just heard Michael asked Sara to go to the party instead of me.

53 Breaking a mirror

It was long believed that a person's reflection showed the soul and that to break the reflection was to harm the soul. So a person who breaks a mirror and damages the reflection it gives will have seven years bad luck.

A: What happened to that beautiful mirror you had hanging by the table?

B: I broke it when I was cleaning.

A: Oh, no! Seven years is a long time to have bad luck.

54 Putting a button in the wrong hole

According to tradition, incorrectly closing the buttons on your clothes will bring misfortune. The only way to protect yourself is to take off the clothes and start over again.

A: I was in such a hurry to get to work this morning that I couldn't even button my shirt. I had to take it off and start over three times.

B: Why did you take it off?

A: Today I'm going to meet my new boss, and I want to be sure he likes me.

55 Destroying a spiderweb

An old story says a spider made a web to hide the baby Jesus from King Herod's soldiers when they came to kill him. For this reason, it is unlucky to destroy a spiderweb.

Mario cleaned his whole house before his parents came to visit. But because he was going to ask them for money to buy a car, he refused to destroy the spiderwebs in the bedroom.

56 Placing shoes on a table

Placing shoes on a table is a reminder of death by hanging, since criminals were often hanged while still wearing their shoes. Now placing shoes on a table is believed to invite a family argument or even death.

A: Are you trying to cause trouble?
B: What did I do?
A: You put your shoes on the kitchen table. Mother won't like that.
B: But the shoes are clean, and I don't want to forget them tomorrow.
A: I smell an argument coming on.

57 Getting up on the wrong side of the bed

Since most people are right-handed, starting from the right has always been considered better than starting from the left. We often say that a person who is quarrelsome must have gotten up on the wrong side—that is, the left side—of the bed.

A: Don't give me any trouble. Just get ready to go.
B: OK. Just as soon as I've had a cup of coffee.
A: No! I want you to get ready now!
B: Wow, you must have gotten up on the wrong side of the bed this morning.

58 Giving a knife as a gift

Because knives and scissors have sharp cutting edges, it's bad luck to give either as a gift to a friend. To prevent "cutting" the friendship between two people, the receiver should "buy" the knife or scissors with a small coin.

Jim was excited when his friend Bob gave him a new hunting knife. But he was disappointed when Bob said he would no longer go hunting with him. "I should have paid him for the knife," Jim said.

59 Killing a spider

Tradition says that it is unlucky to kill a spider. This custom comes from the time when the population of flies, which carried sickness, was kept down only by spiders.

A: I'm not going to visit my grandmother again until she moves to a new house.
B: Why not?
A: Because I hate spiders, and they are everywhere in her house. She won't let me kill them because she says it brings bad luck. So no more visits from me.

60 Opening an umbrella

Since the umbrella was first used to protect a person from the sun, it is an insult to the sun to open an umbrella indoors. To do so will bring bad luck to anyone who lives in the house.

A: Why do you keep opening and closing your umbrella? Do you think it's going to rain inside the house?

B: No. I couldn't get it to open the last time it rained. I'm trying to fix it.

A: Well, to protect us all, fix it outdoors.

61 Hanging clothes from a doorknob

An old custom was to hang clothes from a doorknob of a house or room as a sign that someone inside had died. When there has been no death, hanging clothes from a doorknob would invite misfortune.

A: Please take your coat off the door and put it away.
B: But I always hang my coat on the doorknob.
A: Not today. I'm making dinner for my friends, and I want everything to go well.

62 Stepping on a shadow

It is believed that a shadow represents a person's soul. So any harm that comes to the shadow will also come to the person who makes it.

Carlos was so angry after Beatriz won the game that he followed her home and threw rocks at her shadow. But she still beat him the next time they played.

Section Six
Lots of Luck

63 Finding a four-leaf clover

The four-leaf clover is one of the most valuable of all good luck charms. The parts of the leaf represent four parts of life: fame, wealth, love, and health. The owner of the clover will have good fortune in all four.

A: On the day I married, my mother gave me this lucky clover. Today I'm giving it to you.

B: Now I'm the happiest girl in the world and the luckiest, too.

64 Wearing an acorn

Because the strong oak tree, which grows from a little acorn, lives for such a long time, it is believed that wearing an acorn as a charm will bring good luck and a long life.

A: What's that on your necklace?
B: A gold acorn. I was wearing this when I met my husband. It always brings me luck.

65 Hanging a horseshoe over the door

A horseshoe has always been considered a good luck charm. Some say this is because the horseshoe is in the shape of a half moon, a symbol of good fortune. Horseshoes often are hung over the door of a house or barn for protection.

A: How do you like our new house? We'll be moving in next week.
B: It needs just one more thing for the finishing touch. I brought you this horseshoe to hang over the door.

66 Carrying a rabbit's foot

One of the most common good luck charms is a rabbit's foot. It is considered lucky because rabbits have many offspring, and having many children is a sign of wealth.

A: Are you ready for the big test in math today?
B: Yes. I didn't study much, but I've got my rabbit's foot right here.

67 Saying "Break a leg" to an actor

Sometimes we must try to trick any evil spirits that might be listening. Wishing an actor "good luck" before he goes onstage is believed to be an invitation for bad things to happen. Instead, a person should tell the actor to "break a leg" because by wishing for a bad thing, good luck will come.

A: I've never had such a big part in a play before. Wish me luck.
B: Go out there and break a leg!

68 Wearing a ring in one's ear

According to tradition, rings have many magical powers. Making a hole through the earlobe was a way to let out harmful spirits that might have entered the body. Putting a ring through the hole would bring good luck and a long life.

A: Phil must be the luckiest guy in the world.
B: Why do you think so?
A: He's got three holes in each ear and a ring in every one.

69 Picking up a pin

Pins are considered magical because they are made from shiny metal. Superstition says it is lucky to find a pin on the floor and pick it up.

> See a pin, pick it up.
> All the day you'll have good luck.

Lisa was excited about the new dress her mother was making for her birthday. She knew the day would be perfect when she picked up four pins from the sewing room floor. And in fact, when she got home, her parents gave her a fantastic birthday present—a ticket and some spending money for a vacation in Europe.

70 Knocking on wood

People once believed that the spirits of the gods lived in trees. So when we talk of our good fortune, we knock on wood three times to ask the spirit inside the wood to protect our luck and not to punish us for praising ourselves.

A: I've been sick all winter.
B: Not me, knock on wood. My whole family has stayed healthy this year.

86

71 Making a circle with the thumb and forefinger

A good luck sign may be made by bringing the thumb and forefinger together to form a circle. Since the circle has no beginning and no end, it is a symbol of luck. Nowadays this sign is often made to show congratulations.

A: So did you get the promotion, or didn't you?
B: I sure did!
A: Congratulations! Let's go out and celebrate with dinner and champagne. It's on me!

Section Seven
Win or Lose

72 Changing your luck at cards

A player may change bad luck to good by playing with a new deck of cards.

A: No more! I've lost all five games.
B: Come on! Play just one more. I'll get the new deck of cards.

73 Playing cards on a shiny table

Cards should never be played on a shiny table. For best
luck the table should be covered with a green cloth.

A: This green tablecloth should make my wife happy.
B: Why? Is green her favorite color?
A: No. The game is at our house tonight, and she's been losing
   lately. Maybe this will change her luck.

74 Beginner's luck

According to a common superstition, first-time gamblers always win because of "beginner's luck."

A: I'm not playing cards tonight.
B: Why not? What's the matter?
A: This is Lee's first time to play, and I don't have money to lose.

75 Crossing your legs while playing

A card player must never sit at the table with his legs crossed. He might "cross out" his good luck.

A: Why are you standing up? Sit down and play cards.
B: I forget and cross my legs when I sit still. My luck is so bad that I've got to stand up to try to change it.
A: The only way your luck will change is if you stop playing.

76 Looking over a player's shoulder

If you look over someone's shoulder while they are playing cards, you will bring that player bad luck.

A: Go away and stop looking over my shoulder!
B: I was just trying to see how well you were playing.
A: Well, you're bringing me bad luck. I've lost the last three hands.
B: All right, I'll go. But the way you're playing, I'd be surprised if your luck ever changed at all.

77 Playing for money on a certain day

Superstition says that playing cards before 6:00 P.M. on Friday will bring misfortune.

A: 5 . . . 4 . . . 3 . . . 2 . . . 1. It's 6:00. Let's play cards!

78 Borrowed money cannot lose

Gamblers who play with borrowed money are blessed.
Because of this belief no gambler will give money to
another gambler when they are playing in the same
game or betting on the same thing.

A: Charles, can you lend me some money for tonight's game?
B: No way. I'm playing tonight. And don't borrow from George
because I really need to win.

79 Losing one's temper while playing

Players believe that if they become angry while playing, they will lose the game.

Stephanie knew Janet would lose when she saw Janet throw her ball at the referee. Janet never would win when she got that angry.

80 Whistling at the card table

Bad luck and whistling have always been connected. One superstition says that if you whistle or sing while playing cards, you will lose.

A: I refuse to be Sylvia's partner at cards.
B: Why? Sylvia's a good player.
A: Yes, but she whistles during the game, and we always lose.

81 Lucky at cards, unlucky at love

According to tradition, a person cannot be lucky at everything. If he is lucky at cards, he will be unlucky at love.

A: Beth and Mario are the worst card players I've ever seen.
B: Yes, but they've been married for fifteen years. They're certainly lucky in love.

Section Eight
Special Days

82 Groundhog Day

Farmers began the belief that the groundhog predicts the end of winter. On February 2 when the groundhog comes out, if it sees its shadow, there will be six more weeks of winter. If there is no shadow, spring is on the way.

A: This cold weather is making me sick. I'm glad it will end soon.
B: How do you know about the weather? Can you tell the future?
A: No, but the groundhog can, and he has yet to see his shadow.

83 April Fool's Day

The first day of April is traditionally a day for playing jokes. Superstition says that a man who marries on April Fool's Day will be ruled by his wife.

A: I was hoping you could give me a ride to school this morning, but I see you've got a flat tire.

B: How can that be? The tires were fine last night.

A: April fool! There's nothing wrong with your car.

84 Leap Year

Leap year is the year when February has 29 days; this year is believed to be a lucky time to begin new projects. A common tradition says that during this year a woman can propose marriage, and it's bad luck for a man to turn down such an offer.

A: This year I'm opening my new store, and I'm sure I'll make lots of money.

B: Yes, and this year I'm asking John to marry me. It's leap year. He can't refuse!

85 Halloween

Halloween is celebrated on the night of October 31. On that night ghosts and witches walk the earth. But because the spirits cannot be seen, children dressed in costumes and carrying pumpkins may do the spirits' "tricks" for them. To protect their homes, neighbors must give the children "treats" of cookies or candy.

A: Trick or treat!
B: Oh, what scary costumes! Please take lots of candy, and don't play any tricks on me.

86 New Year's Day

New Year's Day is supposed to be the day that sets the pattern for the rest of the year. Superstition says that whatever you do on this day you'll do often during the coming year. So people make **resolutions** on this day to do good deeds and to take care of themselves.

A: Happy New Year. Did you make any New Year's resolutions?
B: Yes, I'm going to write my parents every week. I began a letter this morning.

87 Friday the Thirteenth

It is believed that the combination of Friday, an unlucky day, and thirteen, an unlucky number, will bring great misfortune.

A: Why are you so late? If we don't go soon, we'll miss our plane.

B: I don't like to tell you this, but we can't leave on our trip today.

A: Why not?

B: I went to pay for the tickets and my wallet was gone. All our money for the trip is lost.

A: I should have known something would happen. Never begin a trip on Friday the thirteenth.

88 Valentine's Day

On February 14 it is the custom for lovers to give each other cards and gifts. Superstition says that the person who kisses you on Valentine's Day will be your lover for the whole year.

A: Today's the day. I'm giving Beth this card and telling her how I feel.

B: If you can get a kiss, she'll be yours forever.

89 Christmas

Santa Claus, gifts, family dinners, and music are American Christmas traditions. Another custom is that to have good luck in the coming year, the first person to enter the house on Christmas morning should be a male.

Each year when the family came to our house for Christmas dinner, everyone stopped at the door. Granddad always came inside first, calling "Merry Christmas and Happy New Year."

 **90** **Easter**

The egg is a symbol of the beginning of spring and is the most common tradition of Easter. Children color eggs and hunt for eggs hidden by the **Easter Bunny**. The celebration invites good fortune in the coming months.

A: How many eggs did the Easter Bunny leave at your house?

B: I found ten; they were blue and yellow and pink and green.

Section Nine
And Many More

91 Setting a hat on a bed

Long ago people believed that evil spirits lived in the hair. Placing a hat on a bed would bring bad luck or cause an argument in the household.

A: Come in. I'm glad you could make it. I'll put your hat and coat here on the bed.

B: Oh, please don't put my hat there. I don't want to be the cause of bad luck for you and your new baby.

92 Placing a tooth under the pillow

When a child loses a tooth, it is tradition for the child to place the tooth under his pillow when he goes to sleep. The **tooth fairy** will come during the night and leave a gift of money.

A: Mommy, look! My tooth came out!
B: It sure did! Do you remember what to do with it?
A: Yes, I put it under my pillow and then get money for more candy so more teeth will come out.

93 Moving into a new home

To stop evil spirits from entering a new home, you should give the family a gift of salt, bread, and water. This custom comes from the times when wandering peoples used charms and spells for protection.

A: Welcome to the new house. Sorry we have no food to offer you.
B: That's OK. We brought bread, water, and salt for good luck and wine to celebrate.

94 Throwing a coin into a fountain

In the old days people would throw coins into a well as a gift to the sea gods, asking that they not cause the wells to dry up. Nowadays, the tradition is that if a person throws a coin into a well or fountain while making a wish, the sea gods will make the wish come true.

A: I give up.

B: What's wrong?

A: Every day for a year I've walked by this fountain, made my wish, and thrown in a penny. But I'm still driving the same old car. I guess the gods don't like me.

95 Crossing a knife and fork

Superstition says that making a cross with a knife and fork at the table is unlucky and will cause an argument. The cross is a reminder of crucifixion, a way of killing criminals.

As soon as Marie crossed her knife and fork on the plate, her brothers began quarreling over the last piece of chicken.

96 Digging at the end of a rainbow

Many think that the rainbow is a symbol of good fortune because it connects heaven and earth. A common belief is that a person can find a pot of gold by digging at the end of the rainbow.

A: That's so beautiful. I love rainbows.
B: Me too. What's even nicer is the pot of gold at the end of each one.
A: If only that were true. I've got a wedding coming up, and I could sure use the money.

9**7** Looking at a full moon

It was once believed that those who looked at the full moon too long risked going mad. Nowadays, people simply believe that there is more quarreling and that strange things happen during a full moon.

A: I don't want to go to work tonight.

B: Why not?

A: Because every time there's a full moon strange things happen in the store. Last month a woman who said she was a witch broke three eggs on the floor to scare away evil spirits.

98 Wishing on a star

Shooting stars are considered to be signs of good fortune. Many people believe that their secret wish will come true if they make it when they see the first star at night.

A: Look, it's the first star. Make a wish.
B: I wish for . . .
A: Don't tell! Only secret wishes come true.

99 Bird flying into a house

A bird flying into the house was considered a sign of death. Birds were thought to represent souls of the dead, and when a bird flew into a house, it was believed to be looking for another soul to join it.

Jill had always been afraid of birds. She believed it was because of her grandmother's stories about birds flying into the house on the day Jill's grandfather died.

100 Toasting when drinking

When the custom of toasting began, the host and guest each poured some of their own wine into the other's glass to prove that neither was poisoned. Later the custom changed to simply touching glasses together and saying "To your health!" to prevent evil spirits from stopping the good wishes of the toast.

A: I'd like to make a toast to my son, Paul, the doctor. May you and your patients have long and healthy lives.

B: Thanks, and here's to your health, too, Dad. One good toast deserves another!

101 Tying a string around a finger

In the old days it was believed that tying a piece of string or cloth around the place of a body pain would remind the person of where that pain had been. Now, we tie a string around our finger to remember something we must do.

A: You need to buy bread and milk on your way home.

B: I'll tie a string around my finger to remind me.

A: And by the way, don't forget to stop at the pet food store for dog food.

B: Boy, at this rate, I'm going to run out of string.

Index of Superstitions